MAGNIFICENT
MAGIC

hinkler

h
hinkler

Published by Hinkler Books Pty Ltd
45–55 Fairchild Street
Heatherton Victoria 3202 Australia
www.hinkler.com.au

Author: Nigel Anderson
Cover Design: Pandemonium Creative
Text Design: Sam Grimmer
Photography: Ned Meldrum
Prepress: Graphic Print Group
Typesetting: MPS Limited

ISBN: 978 1 7418 4808 3

Printed and bound in China

INTRODUCTION

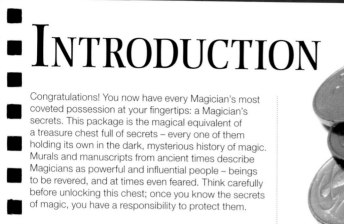

Congratulations! You now have every Magician's most coveted possession at your fingertips: a Magician's secrets. This package is the magical equivalent of a treasure chest full of secrets – every one of them holding its own in the dark, mysterious history of magic. Murals and manuscripts from ancient times describe Magicians as powerful and influential people – beings to be revered, and at times even feared. Think carefully before unlocking this chest; once you know the secrets of magic, you have a responsibility to protect them.

The great beauty of this art is the journey you travel, from learning your first trick, trying it out yourself, and then performing it for a friend. Like a rolling snowball, as you learn and add to your repertoire, your interest will grow. In fact, many people already know a trick – even a party trick – and have fun performing it their entire lives. So just imagine what you can do with the confidential information within these pages!

These tricks are now yours to learn and use, but there are some things you should know. Even a simple trick needs to be mastered to perfection. Even the easiest sleight of hand needs to be rehearsed over and over. It is your responsibility, should you choose to accept it, to promote the art of magic in a positive and professional manner. A poorly performed trick will disappoint your audience, which in turn will be very disappointing for you. However, the good news is that a well-performed trick can be the highlight of an event, the perfect ice-breaker, or simply a great conversation piece, leaving your audience with a strong impression of you and your skills.

You may not intend to become the next Houdini, but who says you won't?

Are you ready to have some fun? These tricks are fun to learn and fun to practice. Most of all, they are enjoyable to perform and to your audience they are simply … *magical*.

Performance Pointers

- A casual manner is a very important part of your performance of magic. You are probably not in a position to adopt a grandiose character of legendary status . . . yet. So be relaxed and enthusiastic, and when you are required to pick up a pencil, dispense with the flourishes and just pick it up.

- Throughout this book you will be reminded to practice your skills and rehearse your lines. Indeed, what you say and when you say it is as important as what you do and when you do it.

- Be sincere when asking for participation from a spectator. Give them credit for the success of a trick. You can still have lots of fun with your spectator. For example, here is a line that always gets a great reaction and a lot of laughs: The Magician looks around the room at the audience and says, "For this trick to work I need someone honest, reliable, and very, very intelligent." The Magician pauses and then points to someone: "That must be you!"

- Most of the tricks in this book include a script. The scripts are just a suggestion to get you started and you may wish to develop your own. In fact, it is highly recommended that you do, as different scripts suit different personalities and different audiences.

- I have written this book from the perspective of a right-handed Magician. If you are left-handed, simply reverse any instructions that refer to right or left.

THE FLEXIBLE PENCIL

This is one of the first illusions all young Magicians can learn, because it is very easy to do.

MAGICAL METHOD, PRESENTATION, AND SCRIPT

1 Pick up the pencil. Hold it very lightly between your thumb and forefinger, a quarter of the way from the end. The other fingers are open.

Your Script: *"I find these rubber pencils quite awkward for drawing. Don't you?"*

2 Move your arm and wrist up and down ever so slightly. If you shake too fast, you will break the illusion. A loose, rocking movement will create the "soft rubber" illusion. It is important that you hold the pencil as lightly as possible – without dropping it, of course!

3 After performing the illusion, drop the pencil down onto the table.

Your Script: *"They are just too soft."*

Performance Pointers

At some point you may use a magic wand for a trick. Many coin tricks use one. You could use the wand, and then – as if it was an afterthought – do The Flexible Wand. Professional Magicians often combine tricks to keep the entertainment level high.

RUBBER BAND SURPRISE

A truly deceptive visual surprise!

SLEIGHT OF HAND REQUIRED

1 Start by placing the rubber band over the index and middle fingers of your left hand. Stretch the rubber band toward you with your right index fingertip.

2 As your right hand stretches the rubber band, all four fingertips from your left hand curl inside the rubber band.

3 Take your right hand away so the rubber band is around your fingers as shown in the picture below.

7

To the spectators, it appears as though you simply placed the rubber band over two fingers.

4 When you open your left hand, the rubber band will instantly jump over to the other two fingers of the left hand. It happens so quickly that it really looks magical.

MAGICAL METHOD, PRESENTATION, AND SCRIPT

1 Display the rubber band and then place it over the first two fingers of your left hand.

Your Script: *"There is something wrong with my fingers. Can you see that the rubber band is around these two fingers?"*

2 Do the secret move and stretch the rubber band over all four fingers (see photos on page 7). Try to remain casual in your actions.

Your Script: *"Watch this."*

3 Open your hand quickly and the rubber band will instantly jump across.

Your Script: *"Don't you think that's strange?"*

Performance Pointers

When you learn and practice this wonderful trick, keep in mind your spectators' point of view. It is better if you are able to do your sleight of hand without even looking at your hands.

THE VANISHING TOOTHPICK

This is your introduction to simple sleight of hand.

This movement is not complicated or difficult, but you will need to practice the technique a few times before you show anyone. The strong impact this delightful effect has on audiences will be well worth the effort.

The trick requires a small gimmick, which will never be noticed by the spectators – hopefully! Combining sleight of hand with a small gimmick like this one creates a very magical moment, and makes your skills appear even more extraordinary than usual!

SETTING THE STAGE

Place the Magician's Wax on the thumbnail of your right hand. Press the thick end of the toothpick into the Magician's Wax. The sharp end should be pointing down your thumb toward your wrist.

A small ball of Magician's Wax is sufficient. This is how it should stick. Ensure the toothpick lines up directly down the middle of your thumb.

The Effect
An ordinary toothpick vanishes from the Magician's hands without a trace. Amazingly, it is then made to reappear right out of thin air.

Requirements
- a small ball of sticky material called "Magician's Wax" (This can be purchased from any magic store. Other tacky products – BlueStik, for instance – work equally well.)
- a toothpick

SLEIGHT OF HAND REQUIRED AND MAGICAL METHOD

1 Place your right index finger over the Magician's Wax so that it simply appears that you are holding the toothpick between your thumb and index finger (see photo below). Your other three fingers should be open, showing there is nothing concealed in your palm. Although it is not really a natural position, it will appear normal to the spectators.

2 Cup your left hand under your right thumb. Your right index finger still hides the Magician's Wax.

3 Your left hand travels up and closes, supposedly around the toothpick. Your right thumb is pushed up with the left hand. The toothpick is automatically hidden behind the right thumb.

Now your right hand should be open, with the left hand concealing the thumb.

4 Close your left hand and draw it away to your left.

5 Keep your right hand relaxed and steady, and don't look down at it! Even if your hand appears completely empty and is in a natural position, if you look down at it, your spectators' gaze will be drawn to it too. Keep your attention on your left hand, supposedly now holding the toothpick. Your spectators will follow your gaze and the movement of your left hand.

6 When you now open your left hand, the toothpick has "vanished." You should appear as surprised as your spectators. Hold your left hand open in a similar position to your right hand. If both hands look the same, it reinforces the appearance that your hands are empty.

7 Now, pretend to see the toothpick suddenly floating in midair in front of you. Reach out your left hand and attempt to pinch it between your thumb and forefinger.

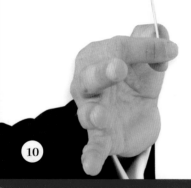

8 Immediately reach forward with your right thumb and index finger and seemingly grab the toothpick from midair with your thumb bent forward and your index finger covering the Magician's Wax.

It will appear that you missed it with your left hand (it *was* invisible), but you got it with your right hand.

9 Your left hand now pinches the top of the toothpick and twists it out from between the right thumb and index finger. The twist helps to free it from the Magician's Wax without any sticking to it or peeling out from between your right thumb and index finger.

10 As you pull the toothpick free, your right hand opens into the natural and relaxed position and you are free to dispose of the toothpick. If you drop it onto the table, you will have ample cover to lower your right hand and "roll" the Magician's Wax off your thumbnail with your right index finger.

PRESENTATION AND SCRIPT

Your Script: *"Did you know that you can get toothpicks made of sterling silver or even gold? This is one of those weird ones."*

1 Perform the vanishing move here.

Your Script: *"You know, the ones that disappear."*

2 Now make it reappear.

Your Script: *"Oh, there it is. Got it! Be careful it doesn't disappear again!"*

Performance Pointers

The first time you perform this trick you may feel that everyone is looking at the Magician's Wax on your thumbnail. In twenty years of performing magic, no one has ever asked to see my thumb or thumbnail during the course of this trick – or any other. The success of this trick depends on your ability to use clever misdirection. Using your eyes, gestures, and body language you should be able to direct your audience's focus anywhere you want (see the photo in Step 5).

THE COIN FROM ANYWHERE

This is perhaps one of the oldest and most delightful tricks in the history of magic.

It is a mistake to think that this trick has passed its use-by date – far from it. With skillful handling and a fun approach, this illusion is guaranteed to surprise your audience every time.

SETTING THE STAGE

Place the coin in your right pants or skirt pocket.

SLEIGHT OF HAND REQUIRED

The technique is straightforward, but not necessarily easy. You will understand how to do it after studying the photos, but it will take practice to perform it with a professional touch.

This trick combines the skillful manipulation of producing a coin from a "finger-palmed" position to your fingertips and an overt use of misdirection to hide the sleight.

1. This starting position is called "finger-palming" a coin. The coin is held loosely between the last two joints of the middle and ring fingers of the right hand. In this position you are able to point using your index finger and your hand looks both natural and empty when held palm down. (A spectator will not suspect you have a coin in your hand because you haven't announced what you are going to do, nor have you mentioned anything about coins.) Hold both hands in a similar position so that you don't have one hand open and one hand closed, for example.

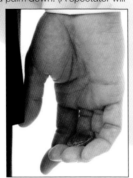

The Effect
The Magician reaches forward and draws a coin from behind a child's ear.

Requirements
- a coin (Thinner coins are easier to use, but bigger coins look better! Choose a coin that will suit your character and performance style. If you have traveled recently, for instance, it might be fun to use a foreign coin. Clean the coin you are planning to use. Sticky coins are difficult to manipulate, and you want your rehearsals and performances to be smooth. And, of course, a clean shiny coin looks so much nicer.)
- clothing with a pocket

2. Use your left hand to point to the right side of the child's head as you ask, "What is that you have there?" Tilt your head to your left to have a good look. Your goal is to direct everyone's attention to the child's right ear.

3. Reach out with your right hand to the child's left ear. When you reach out with your right hand, palm down, your right hand appears to be open and empty. However, if you have directed all the attention to the child's right ear with your left hand, no one will be watching your right hand too closely anyway.

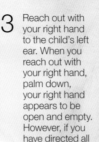

4 Let the coin fall slightly toward your fingertips. Then place your thumb on the edge of the coin (the edge closest to your palm) and push against it, sliding it up the length of your fingers to your fingertips. This action will require some practice.

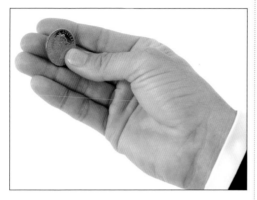

5 Hold the coin between your thumb and index finger, with the rest of your hand open.

MAGICAL METHOD, PRESENTATION, AND SCRIPT

1 Reach into your pocket, take the coin, and palm it in your right hand using the method described above. Draw your hand out, but keep it relaxed and natural looking.

Your opening comments will depend on the age of the children you wish to entertain.

Your Script: *"Do you know which are the richest animals on the farm?"*

(Let them guess as many animals as they want.)

Your Script: *"The pigs, because they're in charge of the piggy banks!"*

2 Approach one of the children. Look to the child's right ear and point with your left hand.

Your Script: *"What is that you have there?"*

3 Now reach out to the child's left ear and produce the coin at your right fingertips. Everyone will be astonished and delighted – especially your young assistant!

It is always interesting to make a few comments after such a quick effect.

Your Script: *"Shame you don't have bigger ears. We could probably find bigger coins."*

Performance Pointers

Remember that you are limited only by your imagination. You could immediately pluck a second coin from your own ear by "finger-palming" a coin in your left hand from the beginning.

The old saying "The hand is quicker than the eye" does not apply here. If you throw your hand out too quickly, you may accidentally end up knocking someone out! Rather, good technique and a fluid action are all that are required. Ensure you have redirected the audience's attention to the child's right ear before you smoothly draw out the coin from the other side.

This classic illusion is not just for children! Many top Magicians use this trick when performing for adults – whether at a wedding function, restaurant, or private cocktail party – plucking coins from behind a gentleman's shoulder or from a lady's elbow.

Magician's Secrets

As in other tricks where a coin is "palmed" (see The French Drop on page 29), if you usually wear a ring on your right hand you should remove it before you perform this routine, or it may "clink" against the coin and give away your method.

The Foam Ball Through the Table

You are about to discover one of magic's most useful and magical items: the foam ball.

Think carefully about where and when to perform this effect. It lasts barely more than ten seconds, so even though it is a terrific routine, I advise you to use it in a "spur-of-the-moment" situation rather than building it up as a major magical extravaganza.

SETTING THE STAGE

Place one foam ball in your right pants or skirt pocket. You are ready to perform this amazing trick anywhere, anytime.

SLEIGHT OF HAND REQUIRED

This sleight-of-hand technique is what Magicians call a "false transfer."

The Effect

The Magician shows a colorful little foam ball. The Magician appears to crush it into the surface of the table – and it genuinely vanishes! The Magician reaches under the table and brings out the foam ball – as if it literally went through the table.

Requirements

- a foam ball (Many tricks in this book can be performed using ordinary items found around the house. However, for this routine you will need to go to a magic shop or make a purchase online. Foam balls are especially popular for kids' magic, and are therefore available in many different sizes, shapes, and delightful colors. When you make your decision, keep in mind that younger children prefer bright colors – especially primary colors.)
- clothing with a pocket
- a clean, flat table to work on

1 This is your starting position. Pinch the foam ball between the middle and ring fingers of your right hand.

2 Place the foam ball into your open left hand.

3 Curl the left-hand fingers up and around the foam ball. As soon as the left-hand fingers cover the foam ball from the spectators' view, you will curl the middle, ring, and pinkie fingers of the right hand.

4 As you curl the fingers of your right hand, "steal" the foam ball back into your right hand. Notice that your right-hand index finger stays pointing into your left hand as a "convincer."

5 Separate your hands and it will appear that the foam ball is held in the left hand. Using additional "convincers" (seen in The French Drop on page 29) – such as relaxing the right hand, or immediately putting it under the table and focusing your attention on the left hand – will reinforce the spectator's belief that you have indeed placed the ball in your left hand.

MAGICAL METHOD, PRESENTATION, AND SCRIPT

1 Display the colorful foam ball to your audience. Allow a spectator to look at it – even touch it. Be aware that if they have never seen a foam ball prior to your performance it may appear to be a very strange item. Make a light-hearted comment.

Your Script: *"What do you think this strange little thing is?"*

Spectator: *"A ball?"*

"It looks like a clown nose. Would you like to wear it?"

Children always tend to say "yes" and adults always tend to say "no." Whatever the situation, this line usually gets a good laugh.

2 Hold the ball in position, pinched between the middle and ring fingers of your right hand.

Your Script: *"Remember how I said it was a strange little ball?"*

3 Perform the false transfer, keeping the foam ball in your right hand, then immediately place your left hand onto the table and your right hand underneath the table. As you put your left hand on the table, you could make a knock with your knuckles for dramatic effect.

Your Script: *"If I take the ball like this and press it into the table . . ."*

4 Your left hand opens and "rubs" the foam ball into the table. Take your time, and act out the motions of making the foam ball go through the table's surface. Then peel your left hand off the table and reveal that the foam ball is completely gone. Avoid comedy or distracting remarks at the moment you peel your hand away. Concentrate on the effect – it is very strong.

Your Script: *". . . it has completely gone . . ."*

5 Produce the ball from under the table, as though you caught it as it dropped through. Roll it in a gentle and casual manner onto the table.

Your Script: *"...and reappeared under here!"*

6 The spectators will definitely want to look at it and touch it now!

Your Script: *"I told you it was strange."*

Performance Pointers

The strength of this trick's effect on your spectators is in direct proportion to the quality of your sleight-of-hand technique. If you put in the time and effort to practice the sleight until you can almost convince yourself that the ball is going through the table, just imagine how amazed your audience will be!

SPLITTING THE ATOM

This effect – how to "split" the single foam ball – fits in wonderfully among other foam-ball routines.

It has been said that one of the main differences between an amateur Magician and a professional is the way in which transitions between tricks are handled. An amateur might perform a trick and then say, "Hmm, let's see what I can do next." A professional will perform The Foam Ball Through the Table routine (see page 13), immediately split the single ball into two foam balls (for this routine), and then move on to a third trick involving both foam balls. A professional Magician uses logical and seamless transitions between tricks.

SETTING THE STAGE

Place one foam ball on the table and the other in your right pants or skirt pocket.

SLEIGHT OF HAND AND MAGICAL METHOD

1   Ask the spectator to pick up the foam ball and examine it. While the spectator does this, their attention will be on the foam ball – and all the other spectators' attention will be on the volunteer. This will give you ample time to reach into your right pocket and load the second foam ball into finger-palm position (see The Coin from Anywhere on page 11 for a description of this sleight-of-hand technique). When finger-palming a foam ball, you will need to grip it quite tightly with your middle, ring, and pinkie fingers so that it cannot be seen by the audience.

The Effect

The Magician picks up a single foam ball from the table. Using a finger as a saw, the foam ball is cut into two pieces. The two pieces spring apart and can be examined as two entirely separate foam balls.

Requirements
- two foam balls
- clothing with a pocket
- a clean, flat table to work on

2   Bring your right hand out of your pocket, hiding the second foam ball in finger-palm position. When the spectator has put the first ball back down on the table, reach out and pick it up with the thumb and index finger of your right hand.

3 Draw the visible ball back toward the palmed ball, in preparation for bringing them out as "one" ball.

4 Use your thumb to help bring the second ball into position next to the first ball.

5 Now place both balls on the table as one, and press them against the table surface under your index finger.

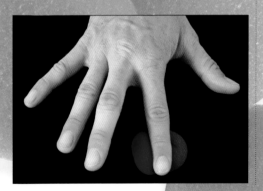

6 Rub your index finger back and forth in a sawing action, and the two foam balls will begin to separate. The effect is highly visual and very striking. It really appears that you are cutting one foam ball into two pieces with your finger.

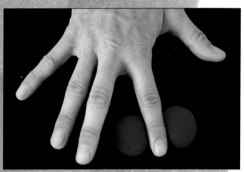

THE KNOTTED RINGS

This is the simplest version of all ring-and-string tricks.

SLEIGHT OF HAND REQUIRED

1 Pass the two ends of the piece of string through the ring.

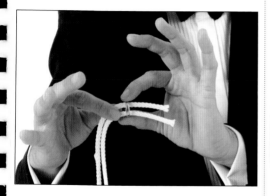

The Effect
A spectator's ring is tied on to a piece of string, and then another two rings are placed on top of the first one. The spectator holds one end of the string in each hand, yet the Magician is able to remove all three rings under the cover of a handkerchief or colorful silk.

Requirements
- a piece of string approximately 20 inches (50 centimeters) long
- three rings borrowed from members of your audience (or any other circular items with holes, such as Chinese coins or metal hex nuts. Use whatever best suits your style and personality.)
- a large handkerchief or colorful silk

2 Now thread them back through the loop.

3 Pull the ends toward the spectator, but not too tightly.

4 Ask the spectator to drop the other two rings over the ends.

Your knot should look like this.

5 Place a large handkerchief or silk over the spectator's hand. Reach both your hands underneath the cover of the handkerchief. Slide the loop down around the ring and all three rings will fall into your open hand. The handkerchief should cover the string and rings from both sides, so you will have to perform the trick without being able to see the knot. In the photos below you can see what should be happening underneath the handkerchief.

MAGICAL METHOD, PRESENTATION, AND SCRIPT

1 Borrow a spectator's ring or use your own.

2 Attach the ring to the string as explained, but don't pull it too tightly.

3 Borrow two or three more rings. Ask your spectator to help you by placing the rings over the ends.

Your Script: *"The name of this trick is The Knotted Rings, which is misleading because only one ring has a knot on it! Still, it's quite hard to do without damaging the rings. The book says that the easiest way to free the rings is with a hacksaw. But there is an alternative method."*

4 Ask the spectator to hold the ends of the string with clenched fists.

Your Script: *"I'll be extra careful today because of what happened when I did this yesterday."*

5 Place the handkerchief or silk over the knotted rings. Reach both your hands underneath its cover. Slide the loop down around the ring and all three rings will fall into your open hand.

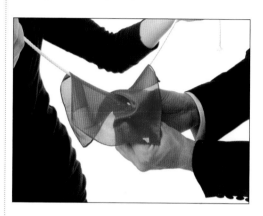

6 Remove the handkerchief and show the rings in your open hand.

Your Script: *"Your ring must have a hole in it. Of course it does, otherwise you couldn't get it on your finger!"*

The Spoon Levitation

This is a wonderful trick that starts out as a simple joke and then turns into what seems like real magic.

The Effect
A spoon (or a pencil) seems to mysteriously float behind the Magician's hand.

Requirements
- a spoon or a long pencil
- a clean, flat table to work on

SLEIGHT OF HAND REQUIRED

1 Start the trick with your left fist closed around the spoon.

2 Grasp your wrist as though you are controlling your magnetic energy. Secretly slip your right-hand index finger over the spoon.

3 Slowly open your left hand…

4 ...to reveal the levitating spoon.

MAGICAL METHOD, PRESENTATION, AND SCRIPT

1 Start by holding the spoon or a long pencil in your clenched left fist. With your right hand, grasp your left wrist and slip your finger over the spoon (or pencil) without showing the spectator (see photo at left).

Your Script: *"Scientific research has proven that our blood contains magnetic particles of iron."*

2 Slowly open the fingers of your left hand as though you really are performing a miracle.

3 Release the spoon onto the table and turn both empty hands face up.

Your Script: *"Science or magic? You be the judge."*

Performance Pointers

There is no need to hold the levitation position (see photo at left) for too long. A few seconds is enough. By offering your spectators a theoretically sound explanation, you provide them with food for thought.

This effect can be done with a pen, a straw, a wooden spoon, a ruler... you are limited only by your imagination. Be creative and have fun.

5 The secret method!

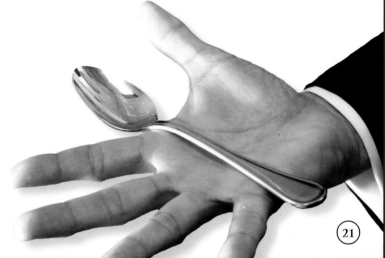

THE HOUSE OF CARDS HOTEL

This is an entertaining routine using a mathematical principle and some cards.

This trick is cleverly presented and has an engaging storyline. (Some Magicians have forged their careers on storytelling with tricks.) This trick belongs to a category of magic known as "self-working magic." That is, the trick works every time without the need for any special sleight of hand.

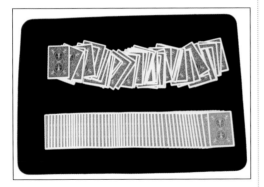

This trick uses a close-up mat, which has a rubber base and a soft felt surface. Close-up mats are available from all magic shops. Poor-quality cards can stick together and can be awkward to use. Good-quality cards fan out beautifully and are much easier to work with.

The Effect

The performer tells a story about a hotel with four rooms and its many guests. The cards are dealt out, then shuffled and dealt out again. Despite the random mixing of the cards, all four Aces end up in one pile, the four Kings in another, as do the four Queens and the four Jacks.

Requirements

- seventeen playing cards (the 4 of Spades, plus four Aces, four Kings, four Queens, and four Jacks)
- a clean, flat table or a Magician's close-up mat to work on

SETTING THE STAGE

The preparation for The House of Cards Hotel is a secret "stacked deck." This means placing the cards in a specific order.

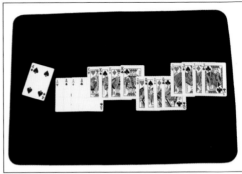

Stack the seventeen cards in the order shown above. Then gather the cards together and turn them face down so that the 4 of Spades is on top.

MAGICAL METHOD,
PRESENTATION, AND SCRIPT

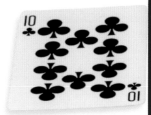

1 Hold the deck face down in your left hand in a dealing position. Deal the top card (4 of Spades) face up in the middle of your working area.

Your Script: *"This is the House of Cards Hotel. It only has four rooms."*

In the following steps you will deal out the rest of the cards to the four positions illustrated as you tell the story, starting with the first card to Position 1, the next card to Position 2, and so on. You will continue until you have dealt out all the cards.

Your Script: *"Four Aces came to the House of Cards Hotel and asked for a room. Since there were four rooms, each Ace was given its own room."*

2 Deal out the four Aces, one to each "room" around the 4 of Spades.

Your Script: *"However, then four Kings came to the hotel and they, too, wanted a room. They were told they would have to share with the Aces."*

3   Deal out the four Kings.

Your Script: *"When the Queens came and asked for a room they also had to share with the others."*

5   Deal out the Jacks. You should now have an Ace, a King, a Queen, and a Jack on all four piles (see photo above).

Your Script: *"It was an uncomfortable night for them, sharing rooms with strangers, and in the morning they all packed up and left."*

4   Deal out the Queens.

Your Script: *"And of course, the Jacks had to share too."*

6   Pick up the four piles in any order, placing each pile of four cards on top of each other. Turn all of them face down in your left hand in dealing position.

8 Now deal out the cards in the same way that you did at the start, dealing the first card to Position 1, the second card to Position 2, and so on. Continue until you have dealt out all the cards. This time your cards will assemble in piles by rank. That is, four Aces in one pile, four Kings in another, four Queens in another, and four Jacks in another (although not necessarily in that order). It really is a great effect.

Performance Pointers

This trick will work every time if you follow the steps outlined here. However, no trick will ever *present* itself, so rehearse your script until you know how to perform it perfectly. You don't want to forget what to say during a trick that is based on telling a story.

7 Take a random number of cards off the top and put them underneath. Do this a few times. This is called "cutting the cards," and the crucial thing is that you are not actually shuffling the cards! Cutting the cards will not change the cyclical order, but to the spectator it will appear that you are doing a perfectly good job of mixing the cards around. You can even ask a volunteer how many more cards to mix (cut) to the bottom. So if the response is "three," cut three cards off the top and put them underneath.

> Your Script: *"They all went on their merry way. I'll just mix these around a bit. How many would you like me to take off the top?"*

You could continue taking groups of cards off the top and placing them underneath for ten hours straight, the trick will still work. Try it!

> Your Script: *"When they returned to the hotel, they decided to stay another night, but only on the condition that they could share with their friends."*

JACKPOT POKER

The most amazing feature of this trick is that your spectator does everything.

If I were to set the most desirable parameters of a magic trick, it would be that I place the cards on the table and not touch them at all during the entire performance. That is exactly what happens here. Surprisingly, the trick is also very easy to do.

This trick is a slightly more professional variation on The House of Cards Hotel (see page 22).

SETTING THE STAGE

1 The first step is to "mark" the Aces. This is one of the techniques card sharks use to cheat! You will use the same method. Use a pen with the same color as the backs of your cards to place a dot in the center of the backs of all four Aces.

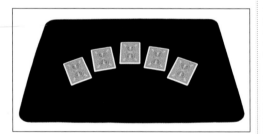

The Effect
The Magician places a dice and a stack of 20 cards on the table. A volunteer rolls the dice to obtain a random number, and the cards are cut this number of times. The spectator then deals five hands of poker. All hands are revealed to show "Four of a Kind," but it is the volunteer who has the winning hand, with the four Aces.

Requirements
- 20 playing cards – four Aces, four Kings, four Queens, four Jacks, and four 10s
- a dice
- a clean, flat table or a Magician's close-up mat

Can you spot the Ace? You should be able to spot the marked Aces easily when the spectator deals them during the performance. You will have plenty of time to double-check because all the Aces will be dealt to the same pile.

2   The next step is to prepare a "stacked deck," similar to the one in the previous effect, The House of Cards Hotel. You need to place all 20 cards in a specific order. The order is as follows, from top to bottom:

- Ace, King, Queen, Jack, 10
- Ace, King, Queen, Jack, 10
- Ace, King, Queen, Jack, 10
- Ace, King, Queen, Jack, 10

The suits do not really matter. For instance, you could start with the Ace of Hearts, then the King of Spades, then the Queen of Hearts, and so on. It is only important for you to have the rank of the cards in the correct sequence.

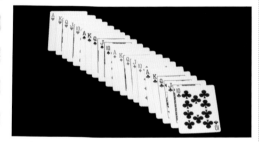

3   Place each finished pile on top of the next, until all four piles form one big pile. Now you should have the deck stacked as shown in the photo below.

The completed stack.

4   Square them up and turn them face down. You are now ready.

MAGICAL METHOD, PRESENTATION, AND SCRIPT

Your Script: *"Many games of poker are played with a reduced deck. In this game you only get four cards."*

1   Place your 20 cards and a dice on the table. (If you do not have a dice, you could simply ask a volunteer to give you a number between one and six.)

Your Script: *"Please roll the dice."*

Assume the spectator rolls a four.

Your Script: *"Now cut the cards four times and complete the cut each time."*

2   You may need to show them how to "complete" the cut the first time and then let them do the remaining cuts. (To complete a cut, simply take the bottom portion of the cut deck and place it on top of the section you lifted off.)

While cutting the deck appears the same as shuffling to an audience, it is in fact very different. Cutting the cards and completing the cut rotates the order, but doesn't change the order. Try it with the cards face up, then spread them out and you will see. (See The House of Cards Hotel trick for a similar use of this "shuffle.")

Your Script: *"Average poker players will often bet with any kind of hand, but the top players only bet with great cards! Please deal out five hands of poker and we'll see who gets the best cards."*

3   As the volunteer deals, watch the cards closely to find where the marked Aces gather.

4 The cards to the spectator's right of the Ace pile will be the four Kings. So push the four Aces toward the spectator and slide the four Kings toward yourself.

Your Script: *"Place your hand on your cards, but don't turn them over just yet. I'll take these."*

5 Turn over the other three piles, commenting on each one. They will be the four Queens, the four Jacks, and the four 10s.

Your Script: *"Well, one of us must have the Aces. Do you feel lucky? Let's turn them over!"*

Performance Pointers

When you practice this at home, you will be amazed that it works every time. In fact, I remember discovering this trick as a young Magician and repeating it endlessly just because I loved the way it worked.

One of the best features of this performance is that the spectator is the biggest winner. Too many tricks set out to make the spectator lose. I firmly believe that if the spectator is made to feel unsuccessful or foolish, they probably won't enjoy the trick very much. So instead, always make them the biggest winner and they'll love your magic even more.

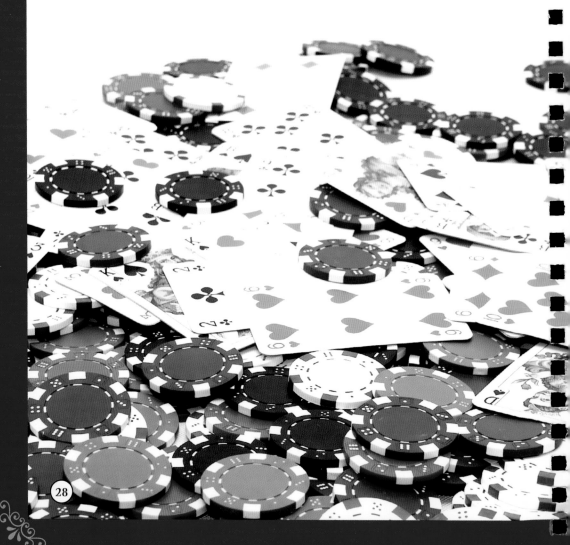

THE FRENCH DROP

If well executed, The French Drop is amazingly deceptive.

The French Drop is very easy to learn. However, there are a few important details that distinguish a good French Drop from a poor one. It was only after a few years into my magic career that I learned how to perform this superb technique in the appropriate way.

A word of warning: Some amateur Magicians perform The French Drop on its own, without a routine. It is presented as a challenge to their spectators: "Which hand is it in? Can you guess?" Of course, most spectators will not be fooled for long. "Well, if it is not in your left hand, it must be in your right hand!" And of course, they are correct!

This kind of approach is too direct, and does not do any justice to this fantastic sleight. So please make use of the routine and suggestions I have outlined here, and you will soon be performing a highly entertaining piece of magic with The French Drop.

The Effect

A coin is held in a display position in the right hand. The Magician takes the coin with the left hand, and a moment later it has vanished. The coin can then be made to reappear anywhere – back at the Magician's fingertips, or behind a child's ear – and then it is dramatically dropped into a glass.

Requirements
- a coin (Any coin can be used for this effect, but very small coins can be awkward to handle. Larger, heavier coins have greater visual impact and are much easier to work with.)
- a wand or a colorful silk
- a glass (optional)

SLEIGHT OF HAND REQUIRED

1   Hold the coin by its edges in the fingertips of your right hand.

2   As you pretend to take the coin with your left hand, let the coin drop into your right hand by raising your right thumb a fraction.

3 Pretend to hold the coin in your left hand, and "read" the date on it. This is a subtlety that will have spectators believing you are actually holding the coin. Don't overact, though!

In the meantime, drop your right arm to your side in a relaxed and natural manner.

4 Continue to pretend that the coin is in your left hand and act as if there is nothing in your right hand. Ignore the coin that is concealed there. Casually pick up an object in your right hand, such as a silk or a magic wand. This subtly reinforces the spectator's belief that your right hand is empty.

5 Run the silk smoothly over your left hand, or tap your hand with a wand. Open your hand completely, revealing it to be empty. The coin has vanished without a trace.

6 To complete the sleight-of-hand routine, decide where you would like to make the coin reappear – the choice is yours entirely. The simplest and most direct method is to transfer the silk to your left hand, and run the silk smoothly over the right hand – just as you did earlier over your left hand. Use your right thumb to push the coin up to your fingertips, or simply open your hand and show the coin – it has reappeared!

Sleight-of-Hand Tips

- Think about how much strength is needed to hold a coin – not a lot. So hold the coin gently in your right hand, and when you "take" it with your left, do so in a natural manner (see the photos in Step 3). A common mistake – made in an attempt to look convincing – is to wrench it from the right hand as though the Magician is wrestling with a venomous snake!

- Another important tip is to believe your own deceptions. Convince yourself that the coin really is in your left hand, and your spectators will be convinced too.

- Remember also that your spectators will always look where you are looking. Ignore the coin hidden in your right hand, and keep your focus on your left hand (see photo at left).

Practice Tips

- Hold the coin in display position (see the photo in Step 1) and actually read the date. Really do it! What does your movement look like when you really take it? This is the exact movement you should be recreating when you do the sleight of hand.

- Every now and again, do the motions "for real" in front of a mirror and then compare them to when you do the sleight of hand. Does your French Drop look like you are really taking the coin? Practice it until it does.

MAGICAL METHOD, PRESENTATION, AND SCRIPT

1 Take a coin out of your pocket or magic case, or borrow one from a spectator. Hold the coin in your right hand and glance down at it.

Your Script: *"Interesting coin …"*

2 Pretend to take it with your left hand, using the French Drop. As your right hand drops down by your side – secretly holding the coin – all your attention is focused on your left hand.

Your Script: *"Made in 2018 … how strange!"*

3 Using natural movements, reach out and pick up the colorful silk with your right hand – still holding the coin – and pass the silk over your left hand in a simple, flowing action. Continue to stare at your left hand. Wait a few moments and then slowly open your left hand. The coin will appear to have vanished.

4 Now take the silk with your left hand and pass it in a similar manner over your right hand.

5 Use your right thumb to produce the coin in your right fingertips, or simply open your hand to reveal it.

Your Script: *"What an interesting coin, don't you think?"*

6 If you like, casually drop the coin into a glass. The audible "clink" adds a dramatic element and a magical touch, and ends the performance cleanly.

7 Everything can be offered for inspection.

Performance Pointers

You will notice that this patter (as with most of the scripts in this book) deliberately leads the spectators away from guessing what is actually happening. The careful scripting steers the spectators' thoughts away from the obvious fact that you will make the coin disappear. They are probably already guessing that's what you intend to do, so why mention the obvious? Instead, say something like, "This coin is dated 2018. How interesting …" By discussing the date on the coin, it is as if you are not even considering whether the coin is here, there, or anywhere in particular.

Magician's Secrets

- Using a coin borrowed from someone can make the sleight even more impressive, ruling out the possibility of a "gimmicked" coin. I have often heard a spectator exclaim, *"And he even used my coin!"*

- Use your imagination to add a theatrical touch to your routine. For instance, use a foreign coin and say that it has mystical properties. Or, pretend you have a "genuine gold sovereign from Blackbeard's coffers" – that would certainly make for an enthralling theme.

- If you usually wear a ring on your right hand, you may need to remove it before you perform this routine. Otherwise, when the coin falls secretly into your palm, your ring may "talk." (This magic jargon means that the ring will make a noise, which will give away the secret technique.)

THE INSTANT SILK STREAMER

This trick has possibly one of the nicest and most surprising effects you will ever create.

Once you have the two necessary items for this trick, you can carry them both in your pocket and perform a miracle whenever and wherever you want to. I would not hesitate to use this as an opening trick, or even as a closer (the two most important parts of a show).

Kids also love this routine because it is cute and colorful.

SETTING THE STAGE

You will need to go to a magic shop (or go online) and buy a "thumb tip." This is a secret container that is shaped and colored like a thumb. Not surprisingly, it neatly fits over your own thumb. The main function of the thumb tip is to conceal something inside it while it is on your thumb. It is the perfect prop for vanishing or producing small items.

The Effect
The Magician's sleeves are pulled up to the elbows. The Magician's hands are shown to be completely empty. With arms stretched out in front, the left hand closes and the Magician slowly draws out a beautiful, rainbow-colored streamer from the left hand with the fingertips of the right hand.

Requirements
- a thumb tip
- a long thumb-tip silk streamer (These are available at magic shops, and come in a variety of dazzling colors.)
- clothing with a pocket

In days of old, Magicians would use small metal containers, such as pill boxes, and paint them skin color. These days it's possible to buy the most amazingly realistic thumb tips. They come in all shapes, sizes, and colors and are made of rubber, plastic, metal, or latex.

Load the long silk streamer into the thumb tip. During your routine, you want the silk streamer to come out of your hand in a long smooth movement, not in a clump, so load the silk streamer into the thumb tip by pushing one end in first, and then the rest little by little. As usual, try it at home a few times before your first performance!

Place the loaded thumb tip in your right pants or skirt pocket.

SLEIGHT OF HAND REQUIRED

Your goal is simple: to keep the secret thumb tip hidden from your spectator at all times. This shouldn't be too hard, because they won't be looking for it.

Start by placing your right hand in your pocket. Put your thumb into the thumb tip (the silk streamer is already folded and hidden inside the thumb tip). In Magicians' jargon, this is called "loading" the thumb tip onto your thumb.

There are numerous ways to start the trick and yet still keep the thumb tip hidden from the spectator's view. You could keep your right hand in your pocket, or just keep your entire hand under the table and out of sight. Four other suggested positions are pictured below.

MAGICAL METHOD, PRESENTATION, AND SCRIPT

1 Reach into your right pocket and load the thumb tip onto your right thumb. Keep the thumb tip hidden (using one of the techniques described above) as you run through your introductory patter. Here is a terrific comedy introduction for children that has been used by many Magicians over the years:

> Your Script: *"What is your favorite color?"*
>
> Spectator: *"Pink."*
>
> *"That was my favorite color when I was a little girl."*
>
> (Pause)
>
> *"And what is your name?"*
>
> Spectator: *"Lucy."*
>
> *"Well, we do have a lot in common. That used to be my name!"*

This introduction works when the Magician is male; female Magicians can make the same jokes by selecting a little boy from the audience.

2 If you wish you can pull your sleeves back, being careful not to show the thumb tip or accidentally knock it off your thumb (which happened to me once!).

3 Show your hands to be empty. Spread your left hand palm toward the audience and open it up completely. Do the same with your right hand, but keep the thumb tip hidden behind the left hand.

4 From your audience's perspective, you are simply showing your hands to be empty. It looks like this is the case. There is no reason for the audience to suspect that you have anything hidden behind your left hand. (Don't attract attention by looking at the thumb tip!)

5 You can now perform another subtle and deceptive movement to show from both sides that your hands are completely empty. Rotate your left hand down to the right, in front of your right hand. At the same time, rotate your right hand down to the left, behind your open left hand. The thumb tip is still completely hidden from the spectator's view, and yet you have shown both hands empty from both sides.

6 Bring your hands together and place the thumb tip into the left hand. As you pull your thumb out of the thumb tip, press your right thumb against the silk streamer and it will start to come out.

7 Close your left hand into a fist over the thumb tip. Pinch the tip of the silk streamer between your right thumb and index finger.

8 Pull the streamer out slowly. One good idea is to pull it out a quarter of the way, and then let your spectator pull it out the rest of the way. Act as though you are just as amazed as your spectator is. There is no need to say anything, or try to be funny – that would detract from this really beautiful visual effect. Remember what your spectator has just watched: your hands were empty, and yet you produced a long silk streamer – incredible! Allow the effect to sink in.

Performance Pointers

In Magicians' jargon, "cleaning up" is the action of getting rid of magical props at the end of a trick. This is important, because once you are "clean" there is no possible way your audience can discover your secret.

First method

As soon as the silk streamer has been pulled all the way out of the thumb tip, encourage your spectators to examine it. This gives you the perfect opportunity to clean up: put your left hand casually into your left pocket and drop the thumb tip.

Second method

After the spectators have examined the streamer, take it back from them and hold one end in each hand. Loosely drape the streamer around your left hand a few times, as if you were casually tidying up. Then place your left hand in your left pants or skirt pocket, ditching both the streamer and the thumb tip at the same time.

Magician's Secrets

Be aware that if you are surrounded by spectators on all sides, you will have more difficulty keeping the thumb tip hidden. Professional Magicians practice with every possible scenario in mind so that they are ready for such a situation. For those just starting out in magic, however, it's important to be in control of your performance at all times. If you *are* surrounded, and you don't feel confident in your ability to perform the sleight without being seen, then change your position, or politely direct your spectators to stand where you want them to.

COIN STORY

An enthralling story delivered with confidence will engage an audience far more than straight-faced patter or even light-hearted comedy.

Some Magicians have forged illustrious careers by combining storytelling with magic. If it suits your personality, then I encourage you wholeheartedly to take this approach. The following story, "Ali Baba and the Forty Thieves," is a charming adaptation from one of the greatest stories from the Arabian collection *One Thousand and One Nights* and it contains many ingredients to entertain children of all ages.

A word of advice for storytellers: Make sure you are able to tell the story without hesitating or making mistakes – because the instant you do, the magical atmosphere you have created will disappear. The technical aspect of the trick itself is not especially difficult. Rehearse the story.

SETTING THE STAGE

Place the four coins in your right pants or skirt pocket. Place the glass nearby.

SLEIGHT OF HAND REQUIRED

The finger-palm is a fairly straightforward sleight-of-hand technique. It will be especially easy for you to load the coin into the finger-palm position because you will do so in your pocket and you will have plenty of "cover." (This is Magicians' jargon for something that prevents a spectator from seeing you do a sleight.) See The Coin from Anywhere on page 11 for a description of the finger-palm technique.

MAGICAL METHOD, PRESENTATION, AND SCRIPT

Your Script: *"Ali Baba was a thief, an honest thief. He was in love with one of the King's daughters, and wanted to marry her."*

1 As you begin your story, be sure to look at your audience and speak slowly and clearly. Roll back your sleeves and then place a glass (the magical goblet) on the table in front of you.

The Effect

The Magician shows three coins with the right hand, one at a time, and places the three coins into the left hand. The coins are dropped into an empty glass. With a snap of the Magician's fingers, the glass is turned over and *four* coins fall out.

Requirements

- four identical coins
- a glass (Even though this glass will be your "magical goblet" in the story, avoid using a glass that looks overly colorful or unusual. To the audience it may appear to be a "trick glass" from a magic shop. An ordinary glass from your kitchen will do nicely.)
- clothing with a pocket
- a clean, flat table or a Magician's close-up mat to work on

Your Script: *"In a secret cave, he had found a magical goblet and three very valuable coins."*

"To marry the princess, he offered her father, the King, the magical goblet as a gift."

2 Reach your right hand into your right pocket and take out coin number one with your fingertips. Show the coin to your audience and then drop it into your left hand.

Your Script: *"He also gave him one ..."*

3 Reach your right hand into your pocket again, secretly finger-palm a coin and *also* take out coin number two with your right-hand fingertips.

4 Show coin number two and then drop it into your left hand, but drop the finger-palmed coin into your left hand at the same time. If you do so in a casual manner and continue with your narration, no one will ever notice the extra coin.

Your Script: *"... two ..."*

5 Now reach your right hand into your pants pocket for the last time and take out coin number three. Show the coin at your fingertips in the same manner as you did for coins one and two, and then drop it into your left hand.

Your Script: *"... three ... very valuable coins."*

Whenever you place your hand into your pocket, draw out a coin and display it to the audience. Make sure your movements look identical each time, so that your spectators do not suspect that you are doing something different on one of the occasions.

The spectators now believe you hold three coins in your left hand, but in fact you hold four.

6 Your right hand is now empty and it would be good to make your spectators aware of this. But, rather than bluntly stating, "Look, my hand is empty!" – which is a tactic I always try to avoid – make use of the context of the story. For example, wave your empty right hand mysteriously over the glass (the magical goblet) before you pick it up.

7 In a moment, you will be dropping the four coins into the glass. It is preferable, of course, that the spectators are not able to examine or count the coins once they are in the glass, as there are still only meant to be three. So, when you pick up the glass, hold your fingers around the front to provide some cover. Ensure your hand looks natural and relaxed.

8 Now drop the coins from your left hand into the glass. Perform this action quite quickly so that the audience cannot distinguish each individual coin.

Your Script: *"The King was angry. He said, 'But I have four daughters. Each one must receive a valuable coin – or I shall chop off your head!'"*

9 Conclude your story, wave your hands magically over the glass again, and pour the coins onto the table, revealing that there are now four.

Your Script: *"Ali Baba said, "King! Wait! I offer you this magical goblet, and to your four daughters – one ... two ... three ... four coins."*

"So Ali Baba and the princess lived happily ever after."

Performance Pointers

Feel free to use your imagination! Create stories of your own or choose stories from your favorite books to accompany your magic. Children will love your performances if you do.

PULLING A RABBIT OUT OF A HAT

This trick is probably more synonymous with magic than any other, and is constantly referenced in popular culture.

Top hats are often used as symbols to represent the art of magic (as are rabbits) – all because of this classic routine. The effect will require more long-term dedication than any of the others in this entire book, but if you ask any child in the world which trick they would most like to see a Magician perform, it will invariably be Pulling a Rabbit out of a Hat!

You can make the false bottom yourself by gluing a 1/2-inch (5-millimeter) "ledge" (made from a piece of foam or flexible plastic, for instance) around the inside of the hat, about 4 inches (10 centimeters) from the bottom. Measure and cut out a piece of relatively thick cardboard, and cover it with material to match the color and texture of the top hat. This must fit seamlessly inside the top hat to sit on the ledge, creating the false bottom.

You will also need to glue or sew a thin loop of black ribbon on to the false bottom, so that you can easily lift it during the performance.

The Effect
A top hat is shown to be empty and then a rabbit is pulled out of it.

Requirements
- a small, gentle rabbit (Be aware that children will always want to pat the rabbit after the show. Make sure your rabbit is comfortable around children and noisy crowds before performing this routine, and always remind the children to be gentle when patting the rabbit.)
- a special top hat with a "false bottom"
- a clean, flat table to work on

When the hat is on the table, open end up, anyone peering inside will assume that they are simply looking at the bottom of the hat, and that it must be empty.

SETTING THE STAGE

1 Place the rabbit inside the top hat and insert the false bottom, concealing the rabbit from view. Place the hat on a table.

2 Place the props for two tricks – for example, a deck of cards and a silk handkerchief – inside the "empty" top hat.

MAGICAL METHOD, PRESENTATION, AND SCRIPT

1 Perform your card trick and leave the cards on the table. Next, ask a spectator to take the colorful silk handkerchief out of the hat and give it to you. This is a great way of letting the spectator see that the hat is otherwise empty, without you actually pointing it out. If you were to say something like, "Is there anything else inside the top hat?" that would, of course, immediately arouse suspicion.

2 Perform your trick with the silk handkerchief, and then leave that on the table, too.

3 If you have any spectators standing with you, ask them to sit down with everyone else. You must be the only person on stage when you perform this final trick.

Your Script: *"In the olden days, the great Magicians could pull all kinds of tricks out of their hats."*

4 Stand behind the table and reach one hand inside the top hat. Use the ribbon to lift the false bottom a fraction and slant it sideways to uncover the rabbit.

Your Script: *"There is another trick in here somewhere, but it is so small that I can't find it."*

5 Look at the spectator who took out the colorful silk handkerchief.

Your Script: *"Did you see any red streamers inside the hat?"*

Spectator: *"No."*

"Did you see any large silver coins inside the hat?"

Spectator: *"No."*

"Any one-hundred-dollar notes?"

Spectator: *"No."*

"Nothing else?"

Spectator: *"No."*

"Ladies and gentlemen, for my final trick, Maximus, the magical rabbit!"

6 Hold the false bottom to the side as you reach your other hand inside the top hat and lift up the rabbit.

Performance Pointers

If you like, you could use a guinea pig instead of a rabbit. Guinea pigs are smaller and easier to handle. You could also give the routine a humorous spin by lifting up your guinea pig and announcing, "From inside my top hat, ladies and gentlemen, my magical bunny rabbit!"

Magician's Secrets

Occasionally I have found that once you remove the false bottom, the rabbit may stand on its hind legs and peek over the top of the open hat. This produces hysterical screams of laughter, especially from children. Continue talking, and pretend that you don't realize that the rabbit is peeking over the top.

HUMAN LEVITATION

Many believe that levitation, or floating in the air, is the ultimate magic illusion.

There are many types of magic tricks that amaze and delight audiences. In this book, I have taught you tricks with cards, coins, and ropes, and tricks using household objects or simple props. There is one type of magic, however, that really stands apart from all others: levitation.

Methods of levitation are closely guarded secrets among Magicians. Some work better than others. This particular version has featured on television and is used by Magicians as an impromptu levitation. It is quite easy to learn, and has the added advantage of requiring no set-up or equipment. I have used it many times and am constantly surprised that it has such a strong effect on people.

The Effect
The Magician discusses the mystical art of levitation, then turns and walks a few steps away from the audience. The Magician spreads both arms and appears to rise slightly off the ground. After bringing both arms back down, the Magician lowers back to the ground and returns to the audience.

Requirements
- black dress shoes (This illusion is more convincing when performed with black dress shoes. The solid heel and the dark color allow for an effect not possible with bare feet, sandals, or brightly colored footwear.)

MAGICAL METHOD, PRESENTATION, AND SCRIPT

> Your Script: *"I have heard that there are monks in Tibet who dedicate their entire lives to trying to levitate this far off the ground."* (Indicate the height of your choice.)
>
> *"I only try to go this high."* (Indicate a small distance between your thumb and index finger.)

1 Walk a few steps away from your audience.

2 Stand with your back turned three-quarters to your spectators in such a way that they can only see the rear part of your right foot and most of your left foot.

3 As you raise your arms out to the side to "lighten" your body, raise yourself by a few centimetres using the strength of your right foot. Keep your left foot horizontal, and use your arms to help keep yourself balanced. Perform the "levitation" slowly.

4 Both heels remain at the same level and the left foot is horizontal, so from the three-quarter angle you appear to genuinely rise off the ground. Remain "levitated" for only one second or so, and then lower yourself back down. Return your attention to the audience.

Your Script: *"Did I go far? I think I went into a trance."*

Performance Pointers

You can only perform to an audience if they are sitting (or standing) together. If you are surrounded by spectators, move to a more appropriate position, or politely ask them to gather together in one area.

Magician's Secrets

It will take some practice to acquire the necessary balance to make this levitation look real. It will also take some experimenting to determine which angle is the most deceptive and also the most "magical."

HOW TO PEEK AT A CARD

In my experience the "peek" is one of the most important and useful of all card sleights.

A huge number of sleights exist that give you the ability to move and hide cards, but it is the use of the "peek" that will create miraculous effects for your audience. The "peek" allows you to peek at a particular card in the deck (often the bottom card), and this card becomes your secret key card. Then you can use the key card principle to perform some very impressive card tricks (see The Key Card Principle, The Police Interrogator and Pulse Detection on pages 43, 45, and 47 for more details).

One of the reasons the "peek" adds so much to a trick is that you can ask the spectator to thoroughly shuffle the cards before you even start the routine. This immediately dispels the notion that the deck might have been prepared.

Once the deck is shuffled, secretly peek at a card. Then you can begin the actual performance.

There are a number of different methods for peeking at a card, but three of the best are described below.

MAGICAL METHOD 1

The first method is the "Tap Peek."

Requirements
- a deck of cards
- a clean, flat table or a Magician's close-up mat to work on

After the cards have been shuffled by a spectator, take them back and square them up by tapping them on the table. It will seem perfectly natural that you are squaring up the slightly messy, shuffled cards. Take this opportunity to peek at the bottom card of the deck, and remember it. This card will be your secret key card.

Alternatively, after the cards are shuffled, redirect the spectator's attention – for instance, ask the spectator to select a card from the deck and remember it – and while the spectator is occupied, use the "Tap Peek" to look at the bottom card of the deck.

MAGICAL METHOD 2

The second method is the "Rotation Peek."

1 Take the shuffled cards back from the spectator and hold them in your left hand. Your right hand picks up the deck from above by the short ends between the fingers and thumb.

2 Rotate the cards from end to end once in a clockwise direction and place the cards back down into your left hand face down. Halfway through this movement, the bottom card will be visible from your point of view, yet the spectator will not see anything at all. A very brief glance is all it should take for you to note your key card.

MAGICAL METHOD 3

By far, my favorite method is the "Pinkie Peek." It is direct, bold, and very deceptive. I created it many years ago, and use it more than any other peek method.

1 Ask a spectator to shuffle the deck, and then allow the spectator to select any card from it. Take the rest of the cards back and hold them in your left hand. Lift off approximately half the deck with your right hand, with your thumb at one end of the cards and your middle and ring fingers at the other. Indicate with the little finger of your right hand (the pinkie finger) where the spectator should put the chosen card and say something like, "Just place it back here."

2 The bottom card of the portion in your right hand will be staring right at you (the 5 of Spades in this example). Briefly look at it and remember it – that is your key card. As soon as the spectator places the chosen card on the left-hand portion of cards, you place the cards from your right hand directly on top of the chosen card. This places your key card (the 5 of Spades) directly on top of the chosen card.

Magician's Secrets

Occasionally a spectator will shuffle the cards with the faces toward you without realizing. This makes your job even easier! Don't let the spectator know, of course. As the spectator finishes, you will see the bottom card of the shuffled deck. Remember it and you are ready to use it as a key card.

The Key Card Principle

A "key card" is a card known to you, either from peeking at a card in a shuffled deck or because you looked at a card before commencing the trick.

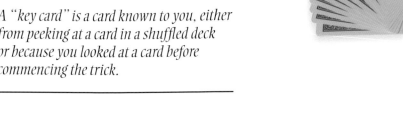

When a spectator chooses a card from the deck, remembers it, and then replaces it into the deck, your key card is placed on top of the spectator's chosen card. It will then be easy for you to locate the spectator's chosen card later, since it will be directly next to your key card.

Here are two methods for obtaining a key card and placing it on top of the spectator's chosen card in the deck.

MAGICAL METHOD 1

1   The most common method is to either look at the bottom card of the deck before the trick starts, or use the "Tap Peek" to identify the bottom card (see How to Peek at a Card on page 41). That card is now your key card.

2   Once you have noted your key card, ask the spectator to select any card from the deck.

3   Next, cut half the deck onto the table and then have the spectator place their card on top of that pile.

4   Now complete the cut, placing the remaining cards (with your key card on the bottom) directly on top of the chosen card.

5   Pick up the entire deck and deal the cards onto the table, turning each one face up as you deal. The card dealt directly after your key card will be the spectator's chosen card.

6   Once you have taken note of the spectator's card, you can use any number of methods for revealing it. For example, as you see the spectator's card passing by, show no outward reaction and just keep dealing out the entire deck. Then declare that a card has suddenly popped into your head, and confidently name the card.

Alternatively, you could try out this key card method in a very strong, ready-to-perform routine I have created called The Police Interrogator (see page 45).

MAGICAL METHOD 2

1 The simplest and most direct method of placing your key card on top of the spectator's chosen card is to use the "Pinkie Peek" (see How to Peek at a Card on page 41). Use this method to obtain a key card and place it directly on top of the spectator's card.

2 Spread the cards face up on the table. The spectator's card (say, the Queen of Hearts) will be directly to the right of your key card (say, the 5 of Spades). Try it now.

3 Having placed the key card directly on top of the spectator's card, it is now easy to spot your key card and identify the spectator's card.

4 Once again, you could now simply reveal the spectator's card, saying that you have extrasensory perception – rather like guessing, but with a strong feeling that you will be right! Or, you could learn the highly engaging routine, Pulse Detection, on page 47, which uses this exact method but hides the technique within the framework of a comical narration.

Performance Pointers

- Peeking at a key card that you later place on top of the spectator's card is virtually failsafe because the spectator inherently knows you never looked directly at their card. It will not seem important to them even if they happen to notice you peeking at a different card.

- Once you have understood the key card principle, there is really no limit to how you choose to name the spectator's chosen card. Use your imagination to create any number of unique routines using this fantastic magic principle.

THE POLICE INTERROGATOR

Over the past twenty years, I have performed this trick all over the globe with great success.

The simplicity of this trick is inversely proportional to the powerful effect it has on spectators of all ages. The subtle use of sleight of hand (the "peek") makes it appear completely without trickery, and the script provides a clever psychological distraction, which keeps the spectators entertained throughout.

Most professional Magicians will use this trick in a close-up environment such as a cocktail party or a restaurant setting, and for the amateur it works equally well in a private home among friends or family.

SLEIGHT OF HAND REQUIRED

The "Tap Peek" is simple and, like all sleight-of-hand techniques, when performed well it goes completely unnoticed by your spectators (see How to Peek at a Card on page 41).

1 Take the deck of cards and casually mix them around.

> Your Script: *"I have always been fascinated by the way police interrogators can look someone in the eye and know if they're telling the truth."*
>
> *"Please give these a shuffle yourself."*

2 Take them back in a casual manner and thank the spectator for helping out.

3 Fan-spread the cards toward your spectator.

> Your Script: *"Just take any single card out and have a good look. Lock that card into your mind."*

The Effect

A spectator is asked to shuffle the cards. The Magician then offers any card to be taken out, looked at, and placed back in the deck for the purpose of testing a secret technique used by police interrogators. While the spectator attempts to give nothing away, the Magician successfully deals the cards out and stops on the correct card.

Requirements

- any deck of cards (A major advantage of this trick is that the cards can be borrowed and shuffled. It makes no difference if there are a few cards missing or if the cards are old and creased. However, if you are using your own cards, try to use good-quality cards out of respect for your spectator.)
- a clean, flat table to work on or a Magician's close-up mat

4 While the spectator is looking at the card, peek at the bottom card of the deck using the "Tap Peek" or "Rotation Peek" (see How to Peek at a Card). The bottom card of the deck is now your secret key card. Let's say this is the 10 of Spades.

5 Cut a portion of cards off the top of the deck and place them on the table.

> Your Script: *"Please place your card here."*

6 The spectator puts the card on top of the pile on the table.

7 Place your remaining portion of cards directly on top, which places your key card (the 10 of Spades) directly on top of the spectator's chosen card. Both cards are now together in the middle of the deck.

8 Begin turning the cards face up one at a time from the top of the deck. Drop each one onto the table and begin your explanation.

Your Script: *"You just need to focus on the cards. If you see your card, don't say anything. Try not to even blink. I'll be watching you out of the corner of my eye. I will notice if you shift uncomfortably or if you react. In fact, your eyes are the best way for me to tell."*

9 Continue dealing the cards onto the table, pretending to watch the spectator's body language and facial expression. If your acting is good, your spectator will have lots of fun trying to keep a poker face or trying to bluff you. Enjoy this part of the trick. All the "work" is done.

10 While playing with your spectator, however, you must keep watching the cards as they are dealt onto the table. When your key card appears (the 10 of Spades in our example) you will know that the next card is the spectator's chosen card. Allow a few more cards to drop onto the pile but don't lose sight of the spectator's card.

Your Script: *"Wait. A few cards back, I noticed a sudden change in your eyes. Your pupils dilated, the iris quivered just a little bit." (Hesitate for dramatic purposes.) "On this card!"*

Performance Pointers

When presented as above, your spectators will be focused on the psychology and body language that you talk about. It becomes so much more interesting to them than just a fun card trick.

PULSE DETECTION

This is the first routine I used for paid, professional work.

I remember arriving at a wedding function for my very first magic "gig," only to find that the client had accidentally booked two Magicians. The other fellow was a seasoned veteran whom I had admired for years, so I was feeling a bit apprehensive. During the evening I performed this effect many times, explaining that I could feel the spectators' pulses and read their body language. At the end of the night the client said many of the guests preferred my "engaging, personalized routines" to the other Magician's "tricks." Needless to say, I was very surprised – but thrilled! I still use the exact same routine in many of my performances today, and I hope you enjoy it as much as I do.

SLEIGHT OF HAND REQUIRED

The "Pinkie Peek" or your preferred peek method (see How to Peek at a Card on page 41).

MAGICAL METHOD, PRESENTATION, AND SCRIPT

1 Offer the cards to be shuffled, but be casual about it. Allowing the cards to be shuffled, of course, makes the trick much stronger, but don't force anyone to shuffle them. Remember that it is always preferable to befriend your spectator rather than challenge them.

> Your Script: *"Could you please take the cards? You can shuffle them if you like. Take as long as you want."*
>
> *"When you are finished, please take one out and remember it. If you have a favorite card, take that one."*

The Effect

A spectator is asked to pick a card. It is returned to the deck. The cards are then spread out face up. The Magician holds the spectator's wrist, and as the Magician moves the spectator's hand along the spread of cards, the cards that do not "feel" right are pushed aside. The Magician continues until only a few cards remain. Spreading these out, the Magician again uses the spectator's arm to "know" which ones to eliminate until only one card is left. It is the spectator's card.

Requirements
• one deck of cards – and a whole lot of showmanship!

Let's assume the spectator takes the Queen of Hearts.

2 Take the cards back in your left hand. Your right hand lifts off the upper half of the deck. Reach out your left hand and offer the lower half of the deck toward the spectator.

Indicate with your right pinkie finger where the spectator should place the card. This is the "Pinkie Peek." (See How to Peek at a Card.)

3 As you peek, ask a direct question, such as "So, is that your favorite card?" or "Will you remember your card?" Let's say the Ace of Spades is the card you peeked at, then that will be your key card.

4 Once the spectator has placed the card onto the lower half of the deck (in your left hand), place your key card portion in your right hand on top of the spectator's card.

5 Turn the whole deck over and slide the cards out across the table, performing a long "ribbon spread" from left to right. You will easily be able to see your spectator's chosen card – from your point of view it is the card located to the right of your key card.

6 If you wanted to, you could reveal the spectator's card now and conclude the trick, but that would be simply carrying out a technique, rather than delivering a performance. To thoroughly entertain your spectator, continue as if you have no clue about the identity of the card. You will find 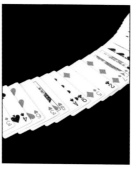 that the best part of the routine is just about to begin.

Your Script: *"Please hold out your arm like this."*

7 Show the spectator how to hold out one arm. (Always show a spectator how you want something done. It will then be clear what you expect, and will avoid any clumsy or embarrassing misunderstandings.)

8 Hold the spectator's wrist with one hand, quite firmly and confidently – but not disrespectfully!

Your Script: *"I am going to use your pulse to find your card."*

"Ah, good … You have a pulse. That helps."

9 Guide the spectator's hand back and forth. It will appear that you are using some form of extrasensory perception. The more you move the spectator's arm around, the more fun it is. Proceed to eliminate groups of cards with your other hand. Begin by eliminating half, then half again, and so on. When you are down to a few cards, separate them and continue to eliminate cards.

Your Script: *"Oh, your pulse is racing now!"*

If you enjoy playing the part of a mad Magician, you may even want to throw the cards wildly off the table, convinced that none of them is the right card! This theatrical presentation can be very funny and keeps your audience's level of interest very high.

10 Finally, lower the spectator's finger onto the chosen card.

Your Script: *"Your hand is telling me … this is it."*

Performance Pointers

Do not rush this trick. I have performed it for a school crowd and it lasted almost ten minutes!

Believe in what you do and what you say. Remember, everyone has a pulse and our pulse reacts to our emotions. So it is plausible that you could use a spectator's pulse to locate the correct card.

COIN THROUGH SILK

The ingredients for this trick are simple and the effect is delightful. Enjoy.

MAGICAL METHOD, PRESENTATION, AND SCRIPT

1 Hold the coin in your right hand between your thumb and index finger, and hold the silk up by the edge with your left hand.

The Effect
A coin is placed underneath a colorful silk handkerchief. The Magician concentrates and seems to use nothing more than sheer willpower to make the coin pass through the silk. Both items can be handed out for examination.

Requirements
- a large coin with smooth edges
- a colorful silk handkerchief, which you can buy from a magic shop or a department store
- an empty glass sitting on a table

2 Cover the coin with the silk. The outline of the coin is clearly visible.

Your Script: To create a fun interaction with a young audience, hold up the colorful silk and say: *"One silver coin!"*

Hold up the coin and say: *"One colorful silk handkerchief!"*

The children will all laugh and yell out that you said it the wrong way around. You may wish to prompt them by asking: *"Did I get that right?"*

Your Script: *"If you put them together, you get a colorful coin!"*

3 Now for the first secret move: pinch a small fold of the silk with your right thumb against the coin. Use your left hand to keep the coin and silk steady while you obtain the thumb pinch.

Your actions and words should flow smoothly together. Even when you practice the technique, you should also practice saying your accompanying script. The script is very important, because it provides distraction while you do the sleight with the silk.

4 Pick up the front edge of the silk with your left hand and raise it over the top toward you, displaying the coin in full view to the spectator. Of course, they are not aware of your secret pinch of the silk.

5 Now for the second part of the secret: pick up both edges of the silk at the back and drape them both over the top of the coin and forwards toward the audience. It will appear to your spectators that you are simply returning the front of the silk over the coin. If you try it in front of a mirror you will see how natural it looks.

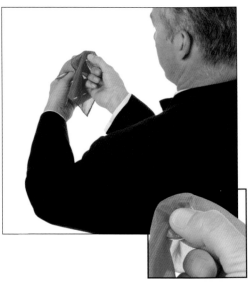

6 You are now ready to perform what seems to be impossible! Pinch the coin and silk from above with your left thumb and index finger.

7 Lightly twist the silk with your right fingertips. This will tighten the silk a little around the coin and provide further credibility to the notion that the coin is well and truly under the silk.

8 Use your thumbs to push the coin gently upwards. Use your index fingers to peel the silk downwards from the front of the coin. Do this slowly and gently. It will seem very magical to your spectators.

Your Script: *"Now I need everybody to blow onto the coin."*

An amusing joke can be to stand back and wipe your eye with your fingers and say: *"I said blow ... not spit!"*

Next, say: *"The coin will now melt through the handkerchief!"*

Your Script: *"Yes, it worked."*

9 Drop the coin into the empty glass. This dramatic sound brings the trick to a conclusion. Open up the silk handkerchief to show that there is no hole in it, and lay it out on the table for inspection.

Performance Pointers

While your spectator is examining the silk, the coin, or even the glass, you have ample opportunity to prepare the items for your next trick. The transition between tricks is what makes a professional show flow seamlessly.

51

THE BOUNCING APPLE

This can be performed with almost any item, and is particularly effective when you use things that do not usually bounce.

The Effect
The Magician, sitting behind a counter, picks up an apple and throws it on the ground. The apple is heard to hit the floor and it bounces back up in the air high above the counter.

Requirements
* a counter or table to sit behind
* a piece of fruit, such as an apple or orange

SLEIGHT OF HAND REQUIRED, MAGICAL METHOD, AND PRESENTATION

1 As you pretend to throw the apple on the floor, your hand will accompany the apple until it is out of sight just below the counter top.

2 At the moment the apple would have hit the ground if you had actually thrown it, tap your foot quite firmly to simulate the sound of the apple hitting the floor. You will need to practice this step quite thoroughly to perfect your timing before attempting to perform it in public. Rehearse in front of a mirror if possible.

3 Immediately after the apple "hits" the floor, rotate your hand and throw the apple upwards. You must learn to do this without moving your entire arm. Instead, use your wrist and fingers to "flick" the apple upwards. Once again, your timing must give the appearance of the apple having bounced off the floor.

Performance Pointers

- Spectators will often frown in disbelief that the apple can bounce, but they are usually willing to believe it for a bounce or two!

- Do not repeat this effect more than twice in a row or your audience may guess (more or less) how you are doing it.

- I have done this routine with a watch, a cherry, a spoon, and even a cupcake. Quickly move on to another trick and the audience will be left wondering how on earth it is possible for a cupcake to bounce so high off the floor.

CUP CRUNCH

Here is a wonderful comedy effect used by Magicians, comedians and street performers all over the world.

SETTING THE STAGE

When no one is watching, place the cup under your left arm, preferably underneath a jacket. You will definitely need to get the "feel" of this position, as it must look natural. Try it at home with as many spare cups as you have. It is actually a lot of fun to practice.

The Effect
The Magician complains of a sore wrist. While rubbing and flexing it, a loud crunching sound is heard. All watching will be momentarily horrified, believing that the Magician has just sustained a broken wrist!

Requirements
- an empty styrofoam cup, or a disposable plastic cup

2   This action brings your left elbow down toward your body and will crush the cup, resulting in a loud crunching noise.

SLEIGHT OF HAND REQUIRED

1   Place your right hand around your left wrist, and simulate twisting your left wrist anticlockwise.

MAGICAL METHOD, PRESENTATION, AND SCRIPT

1 Once the cup is prepared under your arm, do not be in a rush to do the trick. Work on your presentation, knowing that the moment of impact will be very strong.

2 Prepare a few script lines that relate to an activity you enjoy, such as tennis, horse riding, or even magic! Complain loudly that your wrist is hurting. Ask people what they think you should do, and what they would do. If you do ask them, let them answer. Do not be in a hurry to show your trick. The longer this builds up, the more real it will seem.

Your Script: **Then, suddenly, say:** *"I am fed up with this wrist. I know one way to fix the problem."*

3 Perform the sleight of hand so that a loud crunch is heard.

4 It is up to you whether you wish to say that your wrist feels better or continue the joke by crying that it hurts even more now. A good actor would prolong the effect for as long as possible.

Performance Pointers

This is a gag you should avoid doing as part of a magic "act." If you are performing some regular magic tricks, and someone asks you to show them another one, this is not the one you should follow up with. In fact, the opposite is true. Cup Crunch should be performed when no one is expecting any kind of magic or joke. With a straight face, start complaining mildly, and act as realistically as possible when you "crack" your wrist.

THE FOAM BALL ROUTINE

You are about to learn a trick that many Magicians rate as the all-time best magic trick for children.

Not surprisingly, this is also a wonderful trick for adults. It has so many great ingredients: the brightly colored foam balls; a direct, slick outcome; and the fact that the magic happens right in the spectator's hands – all of which make the routine a guaranteed winner. I have performed this trick for over twenty years, and it is the one trick that I know will always be a success, under any circumstance and for any audience.

However, it is not an easy trick. You will need to master the sleight of hand and learn the routine to perfection. This trick is more advanced than either of the earlier foam-ball routines (see The Foam Ball Through the Table and Splitting the Atom on pages 13 and 15).

One of the advantages of this fabulous trick is that the foam balls are so small and easy to carry around in any pocket, you could take them with you wherever you go and be ready to perform this routine at any time.

Foam balls can be purchased from any magic shop, and are not very expensive. They usually come in packs of four. If you are interested in learning and performing magic at a professional level, then this will be an extremely worthwhile purchase.

SETTING THE STAGE

Place two foam balls in your right pants or skirt pocket.

The Effect

The Magician shows a foam ball and places it in one hand. Then the Magician shows a second foam ball and places it in the spectator's hand. After whispering a magic spell, the Magician reveals an empty hand. When the spectator's hand is opened, both foam balls are there!

Requirements
- two small foam balls
- clothing with a pocket

SLEIGHT OF HAND REQUIRED

You will need to learn the "false transfer" explained in The Foam Ball Through the Table. The false transfer is the ideal sleight of hand to use for this trick, and I recommend that you devote plenty of time to perfecting it. Most Magicians perform it with extreme skill and grace, as it is also very useful for coin magic and other tricks.

MAGICAL METHOD, PRESENTATION, AND SCRIPT

1   Reach into your right pocket and bring out a foam ball, holding it between your thumb and index finger. Ask the children if they know what it is. Whatever they say, give them credit for their guesses. It would be unfair to belittle anyone for a poor guess – after all, only a Magician would carry around two red foam balls!

Your Script: *"Please hold your hand open like this."*

2   Ask the spectator to open their left hand. Indicate the required position with your own hand – open and palm upwards.

3   Pretend to place the foam ball into your left hand but do a false transfer and keep it hidden in a tight finger-palm position in your right hand.

Your Script: *"Now, I'll hold this ball,"* (do a false transfer) *"and I have another one for you in my pocket."*

4   Place your right hand (secretly holding the first ball) into your pocket and take out the second foam ball. If you pinch the two foam balls together with the fingertips of your right hand, they will appear as a single ball. This step will require quite a lot of rehearsal. Show the "single ball" to the audience, but keep your right hand moving so that no one can see that you are actually holding two balls. Keep your left hand in a closed fist as though you are still holding the first foam ball.

5   Place both foam balls into the spectator's left hand. The audience will think you are only placing a single ball into the spectator's open hand, and if you act casually there will be no reason for them to suspect otherwise.

Your Script: *"Close your hand tightly, and don't let go."*

6 The spectator will fold their fingers over the balls. Make sure that you hold them in place with at least one finger until the spectator's hand is completely closed around the foam balls.

7 From this moment onwards, you can play up to the audience. You could whisper a silly-sounding magic spell or incantation, ask them to call out some kind of magic word, or ask if the spectator has magical powers. During this audience interaction, I usually move my left fist (apparently still holding the first foam ball) "magically" around the spectator's left fist in a circular motion.

Your Script: Ask: *"Did you feel anything magical happen to your foam ball?"*

Regardless of the answer, say: *"That's strange, because mine . . ."*

8 Open both your hands.

Your Script: *" . . . has completely vanished!*

'Please open your hand slowly."

It is important that the spectator's hand is opened slowly. If it is opened too quickly, the foam balls will spring out onto the floor and the effect will be lost in the confusion. Make sure you emphasize the word "slowly."

9 When the spectator's hand is opened and both foam balls are visible it will be a delightful, magical moment. And very often, the spectator's surprised reaction is also extremely entertaining for the rest of the audience.

Performance Pointers

You may feel nervous the first time you try this routine. If you are under-prepared or lack the confidence to perform the foam ball routine, then perhaps it is best that you do not take the risk – you may ruin your potential to amaze and delight. Instead, choose some easier tricks to perform, and keep practicing your foam ball routine until you do feel ready. It will be well worth the wait.

REAL MIND-READING

If you can master this technique you will never look back, because it may well be one of the best tricks you ever learn.

The conditions of this trick in the eyes of the spectator are incredibly fair. It appears that you only hold the cards for a moment. The spectator shuffles the cards before choosing one and then shuffles them again afterwards. Of the thousands of card tricks that have made it to print, very few have the ability to seem as "impossible" as this one.

The level of skill required for this trick is very high. It is without doubt the most difficult routine in this book. The sleight is complex and will require an enormous amount of dedicated practice – it has taken me many years to develop and perfect this act.

SETTING THE STAGE

A huge advantage of this routine is that there is absolutely no preparation! The cards can be borrowed and shuffled and even if there are cards missing it won't matter. You don't even need to take them out of the box to start. This is an incredible trick to have in your repertoire.

SLEIGHT OF HAND REQUIRED

You will need to know how to perform three different sleight-of-hand techniques: "The Rotation Peek," "The Glide," and "The Tilt" moves.

For a description of "The Rotation Peek," see How to Peek at a Card on page 41.

"The Glide" and "The Tilt" moves are explained below.

1 To perform the "glide," hold half a deck of cards in your left hand. With your right hand, hold the other half from above by the short ends between your right thumb and index finger. You are holding the half-deck up for the spectator to look at the bottom card.

The Effect

The spectator is asked to take a deck of cards and shuffle them. The Magician flicks through the cards, and when the spectator calls "Stop," the current card is shown to the spectator to remember. The cards are neatly squared up, and the spectator is asked to shuffle the cards again and put them back in the box.

The Magician, using apparently extraordinary mental ability, looks the spectator in the eyes and slowly names the color, then the suit, and then the name of the chosen card.

Requirements
• any deck of cards (The cards can be borrowed and shuffled.)

2 Bring the other fingers of your right hand over the top edge of the half-deck as you lower the cards. Your middle and ring fingers should be touching the bottom card (the one displayed to the spectator). Twist or slide your fingers to your right, and the bottom card will glide to the right, away from the rest of the half-deck, and will be covered by your right palm.

3 Reach under the half-deck with your left hand, seemingly to drag the spectator's card midway to the left. In fact, you pull out the second card from the bottom. This is the "dummy" card that the spectator will think is actually the chosen card.

4 To perform the "tilt," keep a very firm grip on the half-deck with your right thumb and index finger, while slightly raising your middle and ring fingers. These fingers will drag the front edge of the  spectator's card forward and upwards slightly, and the edge closest to you will tilt downwards. As a result, a substantial gap has been created between the spectator's card (the 7 of Diamonds) and the rest of the half-deck in your right hand.

5 You can now place the remaining section of cards from your left hand into this gap in your right hand, and square up all the cards. The audience will firmly believe that  the selected card, which was actually the "dummy" card, is lost somewhere in the deck. In fact, the selected card is now the bottom card of the deck. The whole technique looks extremely convincing.

MAGICAL METHOD, PRESENTATION, AND SCRIPT

Your Script: *"Long before cards were used for games like Poker and Bridge, they had a far more important role to play in people's lives."*

"Here, please mix them around."

1 Offer the deck to the spectator to be shuffled.

Your Script: *"In ancient times, cards were used to reveal insights into the past, present, and future, and even into the workings of the human mind."*

2 Take the cards back and hold them in your left hand and run your left thumb down the top end corner of the deck, flicking the edges as you go.

Your Script: *"Now, say stop whenever you want."*
Spectator: *"Stop!"*

3 Using your right hand, slowly and clearly lift the portion of cards from the top of the deck to the exact place where the spectator called "stop." Take the portion of cards with your right hand from above by the short ends, between your right thumb and index finger. Show the spectator the bottom card from that section. Let's say it is the 7 of Diamonds.

Your Script: *"Concentrate on your card. The color, the number, and the symbol. Will you remember it?"*

4 Use the "glide" move to secretly slide the spectator's card away to the right, and use your left hand to apparently slide the spectator's card out to the left. In fact you will be sliding out the second card from the bottom – the "dummy" card. Then use the "tilt" move to merge both sections of the deck back together, and move the spectator's actual card to the very bottom. The spectator will think that the chosen card has gone slowly and clearly back into the middle of the deck.

5 With the spectator's card on the bottom of the deck, you are in the perfect position to "peek" at it. As you finish the action of placing both sections of cards together, perform the "Rotation Peek" (see How to Peek at a Card on page 41). Peek at the bottom card and you will be able to identify the spectator's card (in this example, the 7 of Diamonds).

6 All the "technical" work is now done. Casually shuffle the cards a little without letting the spectator see that the chosen card is on the bottom of the deck. Offer them for the spectator to shuffle, too. You can even close your eyes or look away while you do this, as if you want to make sure that you can't even get a glimpse of any card!

Your Script: *"Please mix them around again."*

7 Now you need to bring all of your acting skills to the fore. This is where a great performer is distinguished from an average one. Don't just "do the trick" and quickly rattle off the name of the spectator's card. Take your time, make your performance a memorable one, and make the "reveal" a believable feat of real mind-reading.

Your Script: *"Concentrate on your card. The color, the number, and the symbol."*

"The color is . . . red. The number is . . . 7. The symbol is . . . diamonds. The 7 of Diamonds!"

Performance Pointers

A professional Magician must always listen to the spectators and be guided by their reactions. Every time I have performed this routine, the audience has reacted so strongly that I have felt it wise to end my entire magic set right there and then. Always finish on a high point. This trick often sets the bar so high that you can confidently leave your spectators feeling like they have experienced the closest thing to real magic.

THE NAMED CARD

This mini-marvel is a great closer and will greatly impress your audience.

I can't praise this type of trick enough. It uses a simple principle but is disguised within a complex routine. This is a self-working card trick. There is no sleight-of-hand technique to master. However, the routine does have quite a few steps to follow and therefore may take some time to read and learn, but let me assure you, it is actually very easy to do.

There is more than one reason why this trick has such an appeal. The first, and most important, is the direct use of the spectator's name. I have performed this at shows and prepared for it by discreetly asking the host for the name of "the woman over there in the black dress," for example. When that woman later saw her name on a card, she thought I was a real miracle worker!

This routine makes use of a "key card," but for some reason it seems to astound even those spectators who are familiar with this magic principle. (See The Key Card Principle on page 43 for more information about this wonderful technique.) After many years of performing this trick, I have come to realize that its strength lies in the fact that it provides the spectator with a spectrum of effects and emotions: their name appears on a card, a bit of fortune telling for fun, counting down the letters of their name, and a correct match to their chosen card.

SETTING THE STAGE

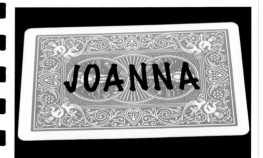

The Effect

A spectator takes any card from the deck, say the King of Spades. The cards are cut onto the table, and the card is replaced in the deck. The Magician spreads the cards face down on the table. One card stands out because it has the spectator's name on the back in large, bold letters – let's say it is JOANNA.

That card is turned over and it is the 6 of Hearts. The Magician explains that the 6 of Hearts represents positive energy and a caring nature. The Magician also points out that the card is a 6, and that there are six letters in her name: J-O-A-N-N-A. The Magician proceeds to count out the next six cards. The sixth card is the King of Spades – the spectator's chosen card.

Requirements
- a deck of cards
- a thick marker pen
- a clean, flat table to work on

1   Decide in advance which spectator you will use for this final routine, and write the spectator's name in large, bold letters on the back of a card with the same number of letters in your spectator's name. In my case, I chose JOANNA, which has six letters, so I chose the 6 of Hearts.

2 Place the marked card with the spectator's name on it on the bottom of the deck, and then place five random cards underneath it. The reason for placing five cards underneath is that you want the spectator's card to be in sixth position beneath the marked card, i.e. JOANNA = six letters.

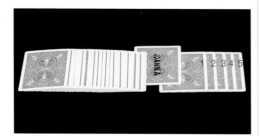

If you were performing for LARA (four letters), you would write LARA on the back of a card (the 4 of Diamonds, for instance), place it on the bottom of the deck, and then place three random cards underneath, so that the spectator's card will later appear in fourth position.

If you were performing for PENELOPE (eight letters) you would write PENELOPE on the back of a card (say, the 8 of Hearts), place it on the bottom of the deck, and then place seven random cards underneath, so that the spectator's card will later appear in eighth position, and so on.

MAGICAL METHOD, PRESENTATION, AND SCRIPT

Your Script: I like to add distinction to my tricks so I often start by saying something like: *"This is a real favorite of mine. It is quite different to everything else I do."*

1 Offer the cards to the spectator to choose from, but hold the bottom dozen or so cards firmly so that your six-card set-up is not seen, and the spectator cannot take a card from it.

2 After the spectator has chosen a card (let's say it is the 7 of Spades), cut a section of cards from the top of the deck onto the table and ask the spectator to place the chosen card on top. Then place the remaining portion of cards on top of the chosen card. This places your six-card set-up directly on top of the chosen card. In this case, the chosen card (the 7 of Spades) will be six cards down from the card with the spectator's name on it (JOANNA).

3 Spread the cards across the table and the spectator's name will be seen on the back of a card. The spectator will be surprised and somewhat flattered. People's names matter to them, so make this an important moment.

4 Take the named card out of the deck, turn it over and say "6 of Hearts" with interest. Try to make one or two pleasant comments about the "meaning" of the card.

Your Script: **For example, say: 'What a lovely card, it represents positive energy and a caring nature.**

"The number six is significant, for two reasons. First of all, it coincides with the number of letters in your name. And second . . . well, let's see what happens if we count down six cards from where we found this card."

"One, two, three, four, five, and this is the sixth card."

5 Turn it over and reveal the chosen card.

INDEX